Bibliographic information published by the German National Library:

The German National Library lists this publication in the National Bibliography; detailed bibliographic data are available on the Internet at http://dnb.dnb.de .

Imprint:

Copyright © 2018 GRIN Verlag
Print and binding: Books on Demand GmbH, Norderstedt Germany
ISBN: 9783668746008

This book at GRIN:

https://www.grin.com/document/427108

Tobias Hinterwimmer

Negiotiating parties of the Cuban Missile Crisis and their strategies

GRIN Verlag

GRIN - Your knowledge has value

Since its foundation in 1998, GRIN has specialized in publishing academic texts by students, college teachers and other academics as e-book and printed book. The website www.grin.com is an ideal platform for presenting term papers, final papers, scientific essays, dissertations and specialist books.

Visit us on the internet:

http://www.grin.com/

http://www.facebook.com/grincom

http://www.twitter.com/grin_com

Structure

- Setup
- Myers–Briggs–Type–Indicators
- John F. Kennedy
- Nikita Khrushchev
- Fidel Castro
- Cuban Missile Crisis
- Conclusion
- Questions

This will be the structure of our todays presentation:
1. We will give you some general information about the Cuban Missile Crisis.
2. Second we will repeat the type indicators which we have learned in the last lesson.
3. Then we are going to describe the 3 main players of the Cuban missile crisis in detail.
4. Afterwards we going to present the course of the Cuban crises and the conversations that were held during the crises.
5. In the end we will give you a conclusion.
6. And if there are still questions left, please do not hesitate to ask.

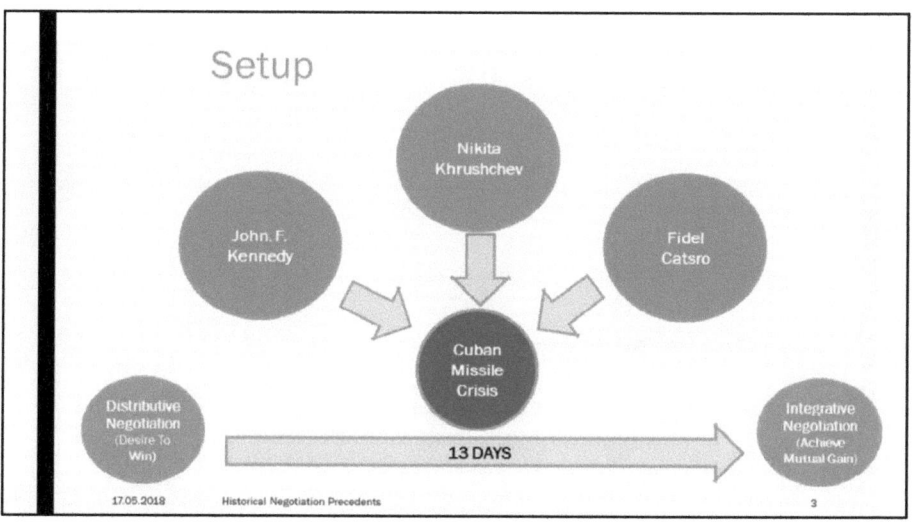

General Information about the Cuban Missile Crisis:
Was a period during the cold war.
A confrontation between the US and the Soviet Union in 1962.
Nikita Khrushchev the Premier of the Soviet Union saw an opportunity to strengthen the bond between Fidel Castro Cuba and the Soviet Union to fulfill his promise to defend Cuba from the US.
In 1960 Khrushchev started to ship ballistic missiles to Cuba
John F. Kennedy then blockaded Cuba in 1962 and forced Khrushchev to remove the missiles

To put it in a nutshell :
The Soviet Union secretly placed nuclear missiles in Cuba
The US interpreted this as an act of aggression
→ Led to intense negotiation over 13 days

3

Myers-Briggs-Type-Indicators

- **Introvert** (likes to work independently and gains his energy from the inner world) vs. **Extrovert** (prefers to work with people and gains his energy from the outer world)

- **Sensing** (more practical) vs. **Intuition** (more idealistic)

- **Thinking** vs. **Feeling** (How we make decisions)

- **Judging** (likes to be in control) vs. **Perceiving** (keeps his options open)

As we learned in our last lesson there exist 16 different personality types which get formed out of those 4 dimensions:
Introvert (likes to work independently and gains his energy from the inner world) vs. **Extrovert** (prefers to work with people and gains his energy from the outer world)
Sensing (more practical) vs. **Intuition** (more idealistic)
Thinking vs. **Feeling** (How we make decisions)
Judging (likes to be in control) vs. **Perceiving** (keeps his options open)

- 1961–1963 President of the United States
- 35th President of the United States
- 1953-1960 United States Senator from Massachusetts

- Interests:
  - Preventing the US from getting involved in a nuclear war
  - Ensuring that communism did not spread to the Americans
  - Showing the world that he was able to face Khrushchev with courage and firmness

General Information:
The first big player of the Cuban Missile Crisis is John. F. Kennedy, the 35th President of the united states.
His presidency started 1961 till 1963 where he got shot during a election campaign journey in Texas.
Before his presidency he was Senator from Massachusetts.

Main Interests regarding the Cuban Missile Crisis:
Preventing the US from getting involved in a nuclear war
Ensuring that communism did not spread to the Americans
Showing the world that he was able to face Khrushchev with courage and firmness

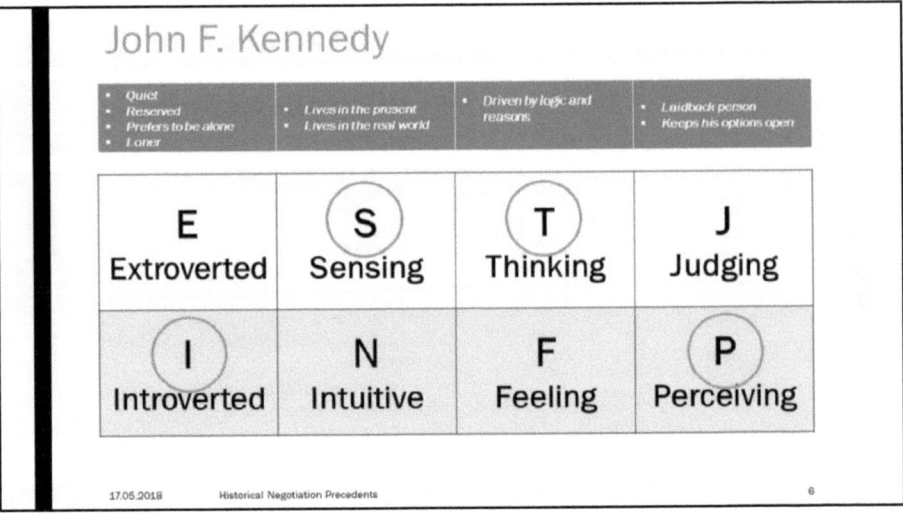

Introverted: President Kennedy would fit perfectly in the picture of an extrovert with a reputation as an outgoing, charismatic person but this picture is not supported by himself, hard facts and those people who knew Kennedy privately.

Kennedy described himself as an introvert, as a quiet and reserved man who preferred to sit in a plane and reading a book then talking to his seat neighbor. Congressional Colleagues said he was a cool or even distant person.

Sensing: He tends to live in the present, but he still had a strong N side because he once said, "Those who look only toward the past or the present are certain to miss the future." Still the N side is not strong enough because Kennedy lived in the real world than in his head or a world of abstract theories.

Thinking: Kennedy was a clear T person who was driven by logic and reason than ethic and feelings as well as his ability to rationally size up situations

Perceiving: Generally laidback person who preferred to keep his options open which you can see during the Cuban Missile Crisis where he listened a lot.

Conclusion: An ISTP can be described as a cool distant loner but with huge charisma. That also explained the fact that he still was pretty successful with the ladies and handled all politic situations like baby kissing and hand shaking very suave. So, he was quiet and preferred to be alone but operated smoothly to get what he wanted.

Contrary an ESTP person, who wants the attention of everyone in a 50-mile radius and think of themselves as a hero, see Donald Trump. Kennedy was a cool-headed crisis responder, which was the best for the Cuban missile crisis. If he would have been a hot headed ESTP person, he took action earlier and underestimated the missile power and provoked maybe the third world war.

<table>
<tr><td>

Nikita Khrushchev (1894-1971)

</td><td>

- 1953 – 1964 Chairman of the communist party of the Soviet Union
- 1958 – 1964 Chairman of the Council of Ministers
- Responsible for the de-Stalinization of the Soviet Union

- Interests:
    - *Did not want to remove his missiles from Cuba*
    - *Remove American missiles from Turkey*
    - *Spread Communism throughout the Americas as well as Europe*
    - *Preventing a nuclear war*

</td></tr>
</table>

17.05.2018   Historical Negotiation Precedents   7

General Information:
The second big player of the Cuba crisis was Nikita Khrushchev. After the death of Stalin, he got the position as the chairman of the communist party of the Soviet Union in 1952. Furthermore, he was the chairman of the Council of Ministers and responsible for the de-Stalinization of the Soviet Union.

Main Interests regarding the Cuban Missile Crisis:

He did not want to remove his missiles from Cuba, because he wanted that America retreats their stations from Germany and Turkey. He could not accept the political position of America – Capitalism has become too close to him. In addition, Nikitas aim was to spread out communism throughout America and as well as Europe.

Nikita Khrushchev

• Impatient • Impulsive	• Lives in the present • Functional relationship to Cuba	• Logical and analytical thinker • Researcher	• Practical • Puts his position in advantage
E Extroverted	**S** Sensing	**T** Thinking	**J** Judging
I Introverted	**N** Intuitive	**F** Feeling	**P** Perceiving

Extroverted: Nikita Khrushchev was regarded as a strong extroverted, because he was an impatient and impulsive leader. He promised his people more than he could deliver (Income of Soviet citizens would increase by 40%/ Only 40 hour weeks). Furthermore, aggressive negotiation strategy with the Americans by requiring the retreat from Turkey and Germany.

Sensing: He was strong communist. Once he said: "Communist scientists benefit mankind – capitalist scientists exploit their people". Nikita Khrushchev never expected a long-term relationship with Cuba, he just wanted to reach his targets.

Thinking: Through that, he wanted to force the retreat from Turkey and Germany. Therefore, he needed a method to reach his target and put America under pressure.

Perceiving: All in all, he felt in the better position, therefore he waited for a reaction of the American side.

Conclusion: People with the personality type ESTP are full of life and energy. This personalities are finding ideas that are actionable and drilling into the details so they can put them to use. Nikita Khrushchev has a compelling sense of himself as a spiritual being who is the searcher and the seeker of truth. He enjoys a fine mind, and is an analytical thinker, capable of great concentration and theoretical insight. Nikita Khrushchev enjoys research, and putting the pieces of an intellectual puzzle together, and once he has enough pieces in place, Nikita is capable of highly creative insight and practical solutions to problems.

General Information:

1959 - 1976	Prime Minister of the Republic of Cuba
1976 - 2008	President of the Republic of Cuba
1961 - 2011	First Secretary of the Communist party of Cuba

Main Interests regarding the Cuban Missile Crisis:
Preventing Cuba from getting obliterated in a nuclear war, Showing his power over the US, Aligning himself with Khrushchev, Removal of trade embargo to Cuba

Main Issues:
rule Cuba without interference from the US => wanted to wage a war against the US with installed missiles + Soviet support

BATNA:
Wait for Khrushchev's orders, fire upon aircrafts & ships of the US using missiles, work together with Kennedy against Khrushchev
=> Castro had a very weak position in the whole negotiation, because he fired at US planes while talks were going on

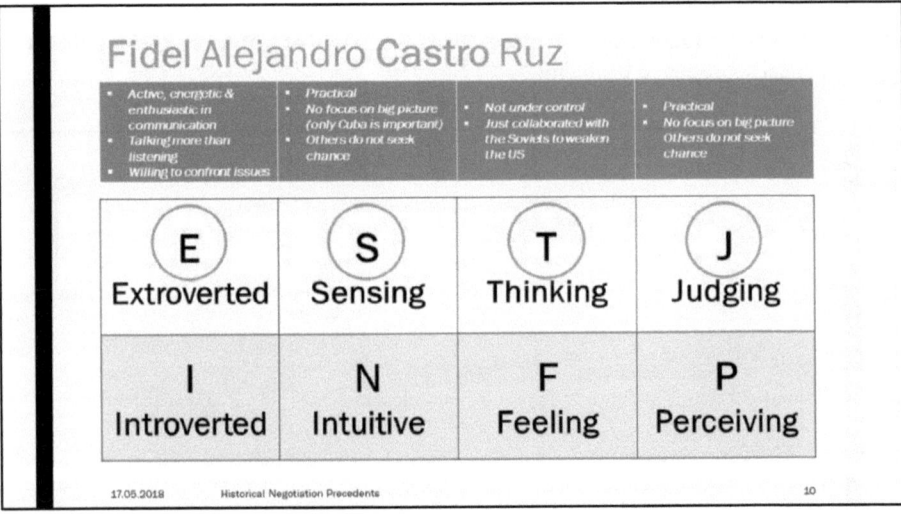

Extroverted: Active, energetic & enthusiastic in communication. He was more talking than listening and extremely willing to confront issues.

Sensing: He negotiated highly practical, did not really focus on the big picture (only Cuba's and his interests were important for him). Additional, his negotiation partners did not seek many chances to state their point of view.

Feeling: He included mainly personal needs (and the ones of Cuban citizens) in decision-making. Furthermore, he acted in terms of connecting first and then challenge his partners (mainly Soviets).
BUT more Thinking: It seemed that most of the time he did not have control over his actions -> just collaborate with Soviets to weaken US

Judging: He acted very goal oriented and decisive. Provided clear expectations from the beginning onwards and preferred control during the whole negotiation phase.

Conclusion: People with the personality type ESTJ are acting extremely active, energetic and enthusiastic by trying to confront issues from the start onwards. Furthermore, they act very practical and as a result of that often loose the view on the big picture by focusing on own interests. Most of the time they do not have control over their negotiation tasks, but instead mainly try to focus on avoiding confrontation by weakening others. In addition, they act highly goal oriented, decisive and provide clear expectations from the day one to gain control over the other negotiation partners.

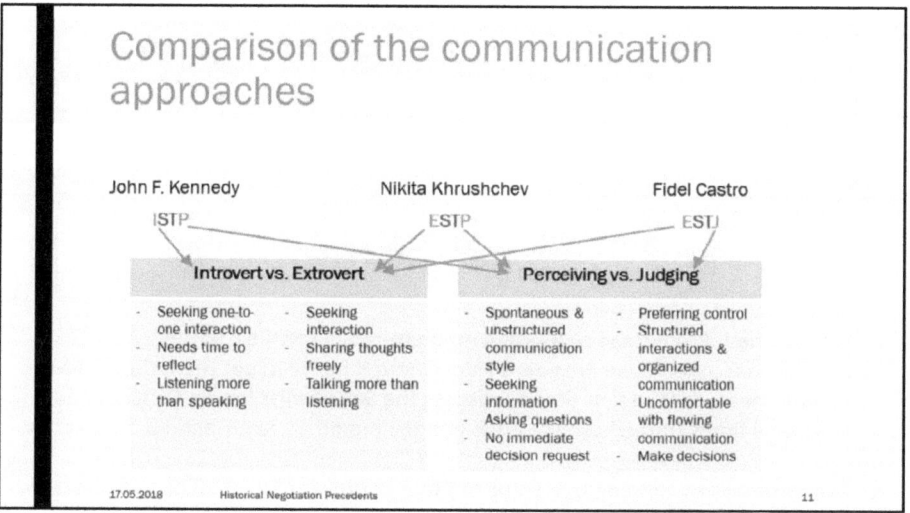

Kennedy <-> Castro:
nearly perfect match for negotiation since two different types (Introvert <-> Extrovert AND Perceiving <-> Judging)
BUT they anyway had extremely different opinions during cuba missile crisis, of course.

Kennedy <-> Khrushchev:
match is not to bad (Introvert <-> Extrovert BUT Perceiving <-> Perceiving)
simillar type indicators => confrontations might occur

Khrushchev <-> Castro:
match is not to bad (Perceiving <-> Judging BUT Extrovert <-> Extrovert)
simillar type indicators => confrontations might occur

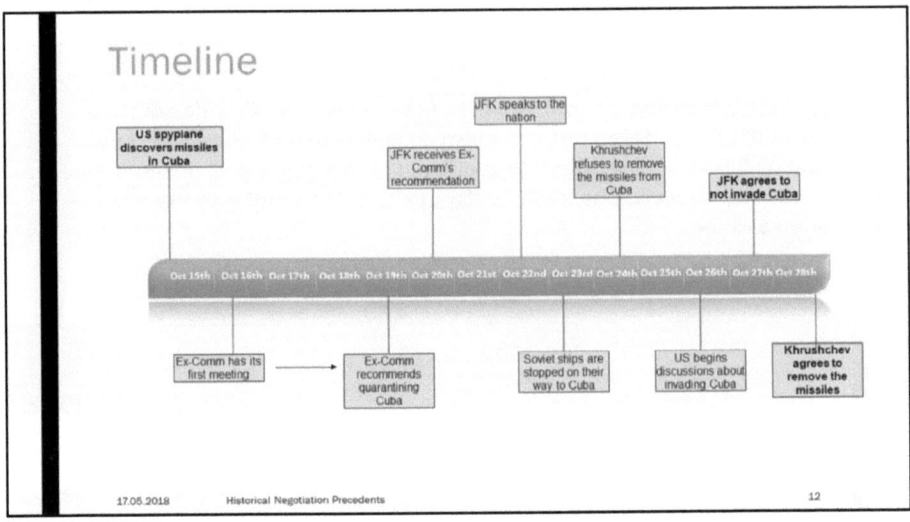

Short timeline about the Cuban Missile Crisis. What happened when?

Only 13 days in October 1962 with a lot of action and the whole world on the edge to a nuclear war.

A **US spyplane takes photos of Russian medium-range missiles**. Soviet leader Nikita Khrushchev has asked Cuba President Fidel Castro if he could put them there in May.

Ex-Comm, meets for the first time to discuss the Soviet missiles. Ex-Comm would meet several times throughout the crisis and the members rarely agreed on what to do.

Ex-Comm discusses sending U.S. ships to Cuba to prevent Soviet ships from reaching the island. They are careful to call it a **quarantine** because a blockade is an act of war.

Ex-Comm's recommendation (quarantine) was given to JFK by his brother Robert.

President Kennedy gives a televised speech to the nation.

President Kennedy gives a speech that is carried live on television stations across the country to inform Americans that missiles have been discovered in Cuba. He tells Americans that he has ordered a Navy quarantine around Cuba and orders the Soviets to remove the missiles.

Soviet ships on their way to Cuba are stopped. This prevents a confrontation with U.S. ships that are around Cuba..

Saying that the U.S. will not intimidate the Soviets, **Khrushchev refuses to remove the missiles** from Cuba. He also accuses Kennedy of putting the world at risk of a nuclear war by ordering the quarantine.

Concerned that the Soviets may not remove the missiles from Cuba, **Ex-Comm begins to discuss plans to invade Cuba** to take control of the missiles.

President Kennedy agrees to not invade Cuba.

After Khrushchev says that he will remove the missiles from Cuba if Kennedy promises not to invade Cuba, Kennedy agrees to the proposal. (He also secretly agrees to remove U.S. missiles from Turkey).

Khrushchev gives a speech on Radio Moscow and says that he has **agreed to Kennedy's arrangement**. The missiles will be removed, Cuba will not be invaded, and the crisis comes to an end.

As we now got an overview of the whole conflict, we are getting a little deeper into the analysis of the negotiations behind it

We already heard, the whole conflict was initiated by the soviets secretly placing nuclear missiles in cuba

Khrushchev tried to use Cuba as means of negotiation with USA to get Allied Forces out of West Berlin and removement of American missiles in Turkey

Castro wanted to use the Russian missiles as a means of preventing any US interference in Cuba

Kennedy's BATNA: Do Nothing (weak) – Diplomatic Pressures (weak) – Secret approach to Castro (uncontrollable) – Invasion (War?) – Air Strike (one of the most strongly supported) – Blockade and ultimatum (best solution)
Blockade: Winning time – get an impression of opponents interests and issues

Neither party has fully understood the others interests and issues in the beginning

Kennedy's speech that he will not back up and do what is necessary

Between two leaders (K+K) it is apparent that they were trying to figure out how they could both retain personal and national honor in relation to each other and to the international arena
Cuban Missile Crisis started out as a distributive negotiation

Phase 2: at least two of the negotiating participants start to realize that they are negotiating about a possible nuclear world war.

This led to Kennedy and Khrushchev realizing that they both had to give something up to allow for a successful negotiation

So it had been the soviets making a move towards their opponent „USA"

Common ground: not to start a nuclear war – Not to lose face – appear like a winner in their home country and to their allies

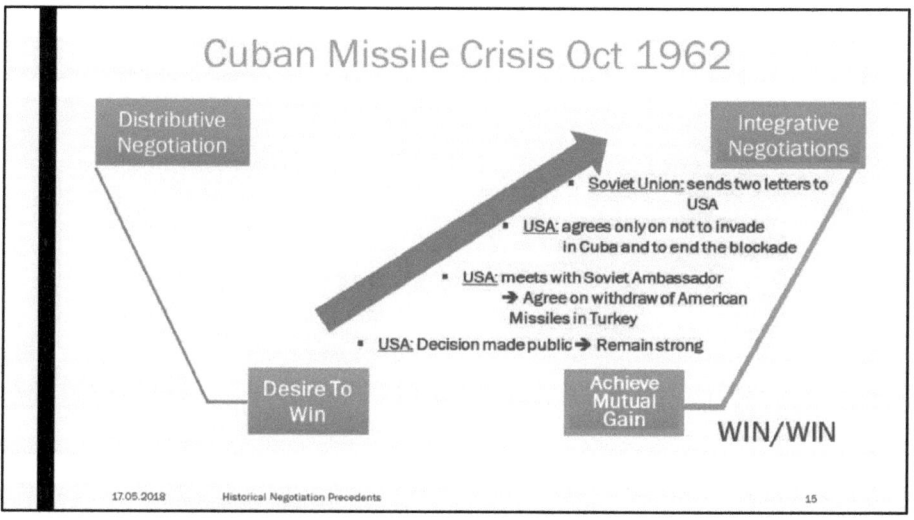

Kennedy showed the world that he was able to face Khrushchev with courage and firmness, unlike in the Berlin Crisis.
Reach an agreement that was integrative in nature and allowed all parties to come away without losing face.

LETTERS:
1. Oct. 26th
Khrushchev offers USA to remove missiles, if the US will not invade Cuba. – Kennedy agreed.
2. Oct. 27th
Khrushchev offers to remove missiles if the US will not invade Cuba, **and** the US removes its missiles form Turkey.
- Kennedy kept the second letter secret from most of the ExComm
- Secret meeting with the Soviet ambassador (Robert Kennedy) to agree to the offer.

- Khrushchev agreed and published to remove the missiles in Cuba via Radio Moscow.

- Only the removal of the Soviet missiles was published, not the removal of the US missiles from Cuba. This made Kennedy a very strong negotiator in the eyes of the American people.

Conclusion

- Win-Win result
  - *Understanding common interest*
  - *Use of private channels and negotiators to conduct some of the important negotiations*
  - *None of the parties lost patience*
- Blockade as balance between observation and action
- Kennedy was was able to control the hard liners in his Ex-Comm as well as external negotiation partners
- Fidel Castro as a risk factor

Rather than following a researched plan, **Khrushchev** acted on **impulse (emotion)** in the **beginning.**

Neither party had a strategy and there was no clear view on how to approach the situation and how to negotiate a solution.

Amateurs are easily led and react to the moves of others – leading to greater chances for concession (Kennedy did not react aggressively ➔ blockade).

Blockade is the balance between observation and action.

Sense makers „act their way into an understanding of where they are, who they are and what they are doing.

Negotiation as a learning process.

Khrushchev showed emotions and lack of control, which gave Kennedy the advantage to act on Khrushchev's reaction.

Logic and reasoning were applied, along with power, threat and coercion, emotion, anger and intimidation.

Sources

- https://www.springtideprocurement.com/blog/2014/negotiation-lessons-learned-from-the-most-dangerous-thirteen-days-in-the-history-of-mankind/
- http://www.academia.edu/5349409/Negotiation_Analysis_-_Cold_War_Negotiations
- https://www.planet-wissen.de/geschichte/persoenlichkeiten/die_kennedys/pwiejohnfkennedy100.html
- http://www.bbc.co.uk/history/historic_figures/khrushchev_nikita.shtml
- https://www.britannica.com/biography/Fidel-Castro
- http://understandmyersbriggs.blogspot.it/p/description-of-8-letters.html
- http://personalityprofiles.tumblr.com/post/145664549506/istpjfk
- http://www.dictionary.com/browse/cuban-missile-crisis
- https://archive.nytimes.com/www.nytimes.com/learning/general/onthisday/bday/0417.html
- http://www.highplainschautauqua.org/nikita-khrushchev-.aspx
- https://www.16personalities.com/estp-strengths-and-weaknesses
- http://www.softschools.com/timelines/cuban_missile_crisis_timeline/108/